8th & Agony

Rich Ferguson

Samantha
All the best
to you!
Rich

Punk ♦ Hostage ♦ Press

8th & Agony
Rich Ferguson

ISBN 978-0-9851293-6-1

Punk Hostage Press
P.O. Box 1869
Hollywood CA 90078
www.punkhostagepress.com

Editor:
A. Razor

Introduction:
Bob Holman

Cover Design:
Geoff Melville

Author's Photo:
Cat Gwynn

Editor's Acknowledgments

In this book you will find a diverse style and approach to poetry and prose writing that speaks of a lyrical lifetime experience not usually apparent in a premiere collection for a writer. Along with the experience, there is the craftsmanship of a songwriter, a modern bard of contemporary musicality. This book is an amble down the open road as well as the dark alley ways and then across a soft beach sand and on into vibrant sunsets that shine on contoured boulevards of dreams both broken and healing.

8th & Agony is a broad tapestry of wordsmithing that has been assembled here in an open parade of personal triumphs and pitfalls that coincide with the scope and vision of a writer who has tuned his work through the trials of performance in a way that has shared this experience with numerous audiences and now has been laid bare for the record here in these pages. Rich Ferguson is a well-heeled spoken word performer that brings a thespian musicianship to the stage along with a storied amount of influence and knowledge of the word, hence the diversity of style and content in this collection. This work is an exploration of poetic road mapping that convenes inside the travelogue of a life experience that touches on all the muses have to bring to bear in this world.

Myself and Iris Berry started *Punk Hostage Press* in hopes of presenting work of relatable contemporary writers that are capable of connecting with an audience based on a life experience that is both enriching and reconciling in its attempt to convey the struggles, triumphs, adversity and even the glory of failures that people go through on any given day. In order to make this type of art more accessible and create a community within the greater community that already exists, we have sought out works that can be used to make those connections more solid. Rich Ferguson has accomplished that beautifully with *8th & Agony* and we thank him for giving us this opportunity to present this book to the world.

We would also like to thank the esteemed Bob Holman for his insightful introduction to this book. The bond that exists between these writers is expressed well in this gateway to the *8th & Agony* that we all meet on the corner of someday.

We also need to thank Geoff Melville for his collage art cover design that captures the imagery of diverse style represented so well inside this book. His efforts have supported *Punk Hostage Press* very strongly and this cover is a definite work of art on its own.

Also, Cat Gwynne for the back cover photo that captures Rich Ferguson so well and compliments the layout of the book design so perfectly.

We also need to thank all the efforts of those who have volunteered time and energy to create *Punk Hostage Press* as a literary arts program that we all hope to expand on in the future. Lee McGrevin and Ian Harvie for all the technical support and promotional input. Sevie Bates for the design input and friendship. Michele MacDannold and Kimberly Kim for the work they have done behind the scenes. Richard Modiano and S.A. Griffin for the feedback and moral support that helps ships reach the shore safely in a storm. Luis J Rodriguez for the inspirational support to make a go of this. Susan Hayden for her steadfast support and promotional work with her *Library Girl Reading Series.* Wanda Coleman and Amelie Frank for being huge

inspirations and spiritual guides. All the writers that we have published so far this year and the writers we are to publish very soon on our humble imprint, *Punk Hostage Press*:
Danny Baker, C.V. Auchterlonie, Yvonne De la Vega, Carolyn Srygley-Moore, Frank Reardon, Dennis Cruz, Annette Cruz, Joe Donnelly, Pleasant Gehman, Sonny Giordano, John Dorsey, Diana Rose, Debbie Kirk, Edaurdo Jones, Puma Perl, Jack Grisham
and Felon O'Rielly.

Punk Hostage Press is a growing family committed to presenting relative works like this one, *8th & Agony* by Rich Ferguson, as well to connecting any and all community with literary arts in a way that builds more community.

We are so very grateful for all of your support.

A. Razor 2012

Introduction

I think what I find so fascinating about Rich Ferguson is his absolute ease with his being.

I think what I find so fascinating about Rich Ferguson is his absolute ease with his being uncategorizeable.

You see Rich, you think hey, it's ok to be a storyteller, so long as you're a musician, and the work looks like poetry when it's on the page. And you got the hat (always the hat), so you are probably a spoken word guy.

And meanwhile the words come at you like it's just a conversation among folks, but then it's like he's talking thunder. Ni, it's that a seed got stuck between his teeth and now it's starting to grow and it's not words pouring out his mouth but all paisley filigree, a vine that leads all the way to heaven and you can climb it because exertion is not physical, it's more like time is swimming and buoying you up as you are lifted into meaning. I mean lifted into understanding. I mean ~ well, I don't exactly know what it means, but Rich he's way past here by now anyhow and I'm keeping up with him so I hope you don't mind if I left you back there with the "I don't know what it means" part, because if I stopped to explain what I think it is to you I'd never catch up with him and he's already in heaven already anyway.

OK, so we will just call him an *artist* and let it go at that. Because he's transforming reality, like a shoemaker with some leather and a full knowledge of foot anatomy. Make it walk, man.

Except that he's really just talking and it's words like we all use so -- well, I guess what I think he's saying is that, as a human being, and he's very sure that that's the species he is of, that he represents, that as a human being, it's what we do, these poem/song/conversation bits/stories. It's like eating, in reverse. It's like the veggies grow in the tummy and then they come lovingly out the mouth to nurture your friends (and by the way, we're all friends, at least to hear Rich tell it) through their ears and direct shot boom like a rocket launch to the brain, a stain on your consciousness that dyes the brain in all kinds of new colors and causes synapse lovemaking and all manner of see-sing so that the real deal will lace you up, not too tight, and you get the purpose: walking. From. Here. To. There.

Over here, where we've already got hold of this book you're holding, *8th and Agony*, this book that I am introducing, that's what we walk towards, one direction of many that Rich's been heading into for forever, or at least as long as I've known him. And that is to say (note use of "to say"), to say that his words work on the page in the same routinized miracle nonstructure that flows like a river of language in his live performances.

That's why his autobiography starts pre-birth in "New Jersey Me":

> It was a nine-month vacation like no other.
> Beat the shit out of Atlantic City
> or the Seaside Heights Boardwalk during the summer.
> Inside Mom's dark-belly Eden
> I was naked and free to do as I pleased.
> I slam-danced to the music of her heart.

That's why when he's making out in a car, the "Down Across Girl" says something like:

> Tear me down with your switchblade mouth.
> Interrogate everything that has been left sleeping in me.
> Find it guilty. Sentence me
> to death. Strap me
> in your electric chair. Shock me.

Yes, it's the poet's autobiography, but maybe more ~ the Evolution of Imagination. Or maybe this is what Everyman realizes is The Truth As You Actually Live It, Sans Bullshit But With a Heart That's So Full That it Speaks For Itself.

This is the place where you are ordered to "Grow Wings or Cease to Be": "a look in her eyes like letting go / letting go of me / letting go of everything / ...one last wish before the ground rushes back up to meet me..." Where you go to "Karma Driving School" where your "fears sneak up on you / like an unmarked police car." And then you "Crash": "crushed by the riot heat, mistaking / ether for Eden / calling upon St. Vicodin / screaming we're in pain again."

Yup, "this is what happens / when you meet your bones for the first time at some party" ("Bones"). " "Christ, how could he even begin to explain all of this? / All this blood, all this money, all this love" (the magnificent movie in a performance in a poem, "Abilene Rising").

I guess this is what you do in an Introduction: Introduce the work to the audience. Fair enough.

Except I could go on eternally blur burping, fart-checking the wonderment of this, Rich Ferguson's first full-scale book. He's proud of it, and I'm proud of him for going this far to get the damn thing written down and bound, which, as he knows best of all, all the while really wants to just be free and fly to you and dance like revolution rhymes evolution with elocution and fried chicken.

And as far as audience goes, I don't think that Author believes in that. To him, we're just one big bunch of gangbangers he thinks of as Family. I don't know who you all are, but I know that the Author knows. I don't know your name but I know his, and it's my great pleasure to Introduce you to the living artist now in lockdown on the page, celebrating the joys of poetry as written word, the text, the product, the printed page –

Ladies & Gentlemen & All the Rest of Us, Too: I'm proud to Introduce you to: Rich Ferguson, the one, the only, the published poet.

Bob Holman
NYC, November 2012

Dedication

This book is for my family (Mary, Norm, Bob, Steve, Ruth) for having instilled within me the right amount of demons, angels, and humor to make it this far in life.

To all my bandmates and loyal musician friends, past and present—David & Jim, Junglebook, Milo Martin, Macho Chris Camacho, Royce, Joel D., Billy Blaze, Brother Jett (R.I.P.), Herb Graham Jr., Jeremy Toback, Butch Norton, Liz Foster, Andrew Bush, Lawrence Manning, Patrolled by Radar, Peter Atanasoff, Rich Mangicaro, Kalani, Michael Barsimanto, Danny Frankel, Lynn Coulter, George Langworthy, Herwig Maurer, Adam Yasmin, Jont, and Bo Blount: I am eternally grateful for all the music and joy you've brought into my life.

To all the fatal optimists that wake up every morning and go to work to earn an honest wage to keep body, mind and soul together: Keep chipping away at every day of your life. And remember, what isn't stone is light.

To all the dogs, cats, snakes, mice, hamsters, bullfrogs and other living creatures that have shared this life with me: I hope that I was as good a pet to you as you were to me.

To all my teachers past and present: Bob Holman, Sid Stebel, Frank White, James Morrison, Rosanna Gamson, Lama Marut, Karen Kochis Jennings, Jonathan Baker, and all the rest: Thank you for bringing your gifts of poetry, storytelling, yoga, singing, performance and Buddhism into my life. I stand a little taller, a little wiser and more fearless because of each of you.

To all the students that I've taught through the years: Thank you for sharing your heart, and your thirst for knowledge in the face of such great adversity. I hope that I've been able to make your lives as rich as you've made mine.

To Crystal Lane Swift and Sadie: Thank you for stretching my boundaries of love, compassion, hope and humor.

To the wide-open highway: Thank you for sharing your breathtaking scenery with me—from the fevered and hallucinatory dust storms of the Mojave to the patient and lush green trees of the Southeast.

This one goes out to all the people that have fed me, shared their stories and booze with me, have let me sleep on their floors while I was on tour.

This one goes out to Jamie Catto & Duncan Bridgeman, Tyson Cornell, Jessica Trupin, Eddie Gomez, Lawrence Mann, and all the other bookers, agents, music & lit-biz folks that have seen something in me; have given me a chance to step up to the mic; step up to my true potential and shout out.

To Mark Wilkinson, Chris Burdick, Andrei Rozen, Gerry Fialka, Ben Staley, Cat Gwynn, Allison Schallert, Aimee Galicia Torres, Luca Dipierro, Zayde Naquib, Victor Bornia, Eric Smith & Ersellia Ferron: Thank you for collaborating with me on such amazing spoken-word/music videos, and thank you for your amazing photography. You all make me look good even on the cloudiest of days in my mind.

To Iris Berry, A. Razor, Brad Listi, Milo Martin, Wayne Reynolds, Brendan Schallert, Kathleen Flood, Peggy

Dobreer, Elena Secota, Susan Hayden, Suzzy Roche, Jane Ormerod, Richard Modiano, Ellyn Maybe, Jace Daniel, Yvonne De la Vega, the good folks at Squaw Valley Writers Retreat, S.A. Griffin, Scott Wannberg (R.I.P.), Daniel Yaryan, Jill Alexander Essbaum, Amelie Frank, Brittany Michelson, Duane Law, Gretl Clagget, and all my other fellow writer friends: thanks for supporting my work. And thanks for not telling me to screw off whenever I've approached you for editing assistance.

To The Nervous Breakdown crew—Brad, Milo, Uche, Wendy, Lenore, Duke, Ben, Zara, Simon, Megan, Erika, Kimberly, Jessica B., Joe D., Jm. Blaine, Joel F., Nick, Rachel, Brother Reno, Greg & Claire, Gina F., Greg Olear, Jonathan Evison, and all the other wonderful writers so numerous to mention that it would take the rest of this book to list your names: Thank you for helping to build such a wonderful literary community in the dark depths of cyberspace.

Finally, to all my brothers and sisters—be you of the blood, the beat, or bringers of light: Let us lift our voices high. Let our words be strong enough and bold enough to lift up not only our own lives, but also the sky.

Rich Ferguson
Los Angeles, November 2012

Previously Published Poems:

"Because of Camp," "All The Times," "Transition into Turbulence," "Karma Driving School," and other pieces were previously published on The Nervous Breakdown (www.thenervousbreakdown.com).

"Abilene Rising," *Oyster Boy Review*.

"See How We Are," *It's Animal But Merciful* (great weather for media).

"The Los Angeles Book of the Dead," *L.A. Times*.

"Hymn," *Onyx Spoken Word: A Celebration of the L.A. Scene* (Projector Press)

"No Animals or Insects Were Tortured or Killed in the Making of This Poem," *Sparring With Beatnik Ghosts Anthology, Vol. 2 - Issue 1* (Editor: Daniel Yaryan)

Table of Contents

Origins & Sin

Journey & Suffering

Destiny & Enlightenment

"Extinguish my eyes, I'll go on seeing you. And without feet, I can make my way to you, without a mouth I can swear your name."
-Rilke

"If you were still around I'd tear into your fear...I'd turn you facing the wind...Chew the back of your head til you opened your mouth to this life."
-Sam Shepard

Origins & Sin

New Jersey Me

Most of my life has been spent in the dark:
drinking in bars, sitting in strip clubs,
sleeping, fucking, searching the black sky
for UFOs. You name it.
That's Me. Lights Out Me.
Searching For Other Forms Of Life Me.

Some of my best dark moments
were in my mother's womb.
It was a nine-month vacation like no other.
Beat the shit out of Atlantic City
or the Seaside Heights Boardwalk during the summer.
Inside Mom's dark-belly Eden
I was naked and free to do as I pleased.
I slam-danced to the music of her heart.
Slow danced to her easy sleeping breath.
With fistfuls of blood and placenta
I scrawled graffiti all over the walls of her insides.

I couldn't help myself. Was out of my mind with delight.
Made crazy by the bitter fruits of her vices.

Whatever she smoked I smoked.
Whatever she drank I drank.
Didn't care for the Virginia Slims or Yuban coffee, though.
All that menthol and bitter grounds made
Fetus Me ball up even tighter.
Kick out of time with her heart.
But the occasional Bloody Mary and sedatives
were another story. In that amniotic ambrosia
I was a fixed constellation of hyper-illuminated joy.

Star Me. Super Nova Me.
All around me spun fiery planets,
frozen wastelands.

Nothing could throw me out of orbit.
Not even those times
Mom would crank the radio
blasting Top 100 crap like "Build Me Up Buttercup"
while cleaning the house; or those days I'd tremble
in time with the erratic changes of her pulse
as she'd sit alone in her bedroom,
praying and crying
to St. Jude.

That's how it was back then. That's how I began
to sense the world outside me, all around me.
For days I'd sit with my newly formed ear
pressed against the inside of Mom's belly,
listening to our small-town Jersey life.

There were the hacking coughs and slurred voices
from what I later saw were the crusty old men
spending their days, drinking and trading fishing tales
down at the marina; the bitching about high prices
and home life from the bent-back blue hairs
shuffling through the aisles of Shop-Rite supermarket;
the tired old gossip about friends, enemies,
and who's doing who
between lip smacks of gum
from the acne-splattered teenage girls
ditching school to hang out in front of the 7-11.

From where I sat,
so many things about my future life

added up to nothing more
than a Hit Parade of Boredom
bleeding into my dark Eden.

That boredom: it was everywhere.

I could hear it in the muffled voices
of medical center workers, cashiers, and
waitresses. Could feel it in the way
my parents spoke to each other, touched each other
before drifting off to sleep. The boredom crowded up
against Mom's belly, worked its way inside.

I exchanged her oxygen for that dullness and distress.
Fed myself on it non-stop. Tried preparing myself
for life in Blackwater:
a little South Jersey coastal town
with no huge malls, libraries, or record stores.
Only hot rods, alcohol, and a strip club–
all the things to make you spin faster
or slower around the boredom.

An even greater threat than the boredom
was the Crab Creek Nuclear Power Plant.
Its invisible doses of radioactive waste
emitted into the air
seeped through Mom's skin.
Those tiny isotopes made me tingle,
gave me headaches.

The poison blended with my parents' DNA–
twisted helixes of my old man's rage,
Mother's fear, married despair–
to form my tiny hands, feet, spine, and brown eyes.

And while each and every part of me was the correct size
and in the correct place, I still didn't feel completely right:

Human Waste Dump Me.
Emotional Frankenstein Me.
I felt almost as toxic as the Jersey
I'd soon be dropped into.

As my senses continued developing
so did my understanding of my parents.
I tasted the bitterness
of Mom's mounting worries and fears.
Shivered to her coldness and distances.
With my old man,
my nose flared from the dank, sulfurous spark
of his anger
whenever he'd press close to Mom
going off about her absences, or how he'd been
busting his ass at work to care for her.

In response, I'd ball up tighter
as if to vanish.
I already knew that, once born,
no matter what I did–
try to get better grades in school, do my best
to clean the house, or be a more tough and loving son–
I'd never be able to make my parents any happier
or make them love each other–or me–any more.

Still, it wasn't all skull and crossbones.

There were days when, over the gentle sounds
of Mom's gestation,
I heard a different small town:

the hum of crickets and bullfrogs tuning for evening;
the hard-rock acoustics of sudden thunderstorms
and the thunderous revving
of souped-up Camaros and Shelbys
barreling down Route 9.
There was also Mom's slow-honey voice—
filled with a music that not even the grime and grit
of Blackwater could quiet—
speaking to each of her Mary Kay Cosmetics customers:
"With only a few products you're well on your way
to being the beautiful you that you are."

Even better than those sounds
were the sounds of those girls: the sweet dark dwellers
over at Duffy's Bar. Whenever Mom went
with my Chief of Police old man to watch him
down a beer or two, I'd hear those girls
woozily discuss their latest boyfriends
or the sleazy customers they'd encountered
while dancing at the Little Red Dollhouse.
Those girls and their gin and Marlboro ramblings
nearly killed me—
Love Crush Me. Spin the Stillborn Bottle Me.

Rib by rib, breath by breath, all those beautiful sounds
of Blackwater built me. Sang me into being.
With the erratic beatings of Mom's heart
as a metronome, I kept time with the music
of my little town: the music that filled me with hope.

There were other hopes and graces along the way, too.

Like when I'd sense my grandmother nearby, her
warm and loving hand resting on Mom's belly

as she'd say: "I can feel him, Sylvia. You're going
to have a boy. A beautiful baby boy."

There were also those cheerful near-summer days–
full of blueberry burst and salt-air breezes drifting
over from the Barnegat Bay–when I'd kick and punch,
sending Mom to her bedroom window
to rub her tummy and console herself.
There, I'd once again witness
all that real-world light
filtering in through her belly.

That light, shining from
those distant beacons of possibility–Seaside Heights,
Asbury Park, even as far away as California–
surrounded me. Illuminated me.
I'd touch my face, feel myself smile.
With my newly developed voice, I'd quietly count off
the miles between those far away places and me.
Even then, I knew that those distant lands
would serve as future sanctuaries.
Places that would feed me
what Blackwater nor Mom ever could:
loud music,
endless possibility,
and light.

Bright, bright light.

Once Mom's water broke, and her blood rushed over me
it was time to see that light. As I rode
the violent waves of her moans and muscle contractions
toward that light, I thought I was ready.
Ready to be born into Blackwater.

Yet once the doctor lifted me high
into the blinding light, and I felt all the good and bad
of my dumpy little town become my second skin
I wasn't so sure anymore. I kicked and screamed
as the doctor smacked the pain of breath into me.
After he cut the cord, he placed me into Mom's arms.

Through her sobbing, she spoke my name for the first time.

Right then, Tiny Seed Me sensed doom.
Being kicked out
of Mom's dark-belly Eden,
smacked on the ass, and
branded with a name was bad enough.

But being born into Blackwater
had sealed my fate in a far worse way.
Before I could walk
I already knew I'd be running.
Running both to my little town
and away from it.
That was my life back then—
part boy, part lost, part dual-exhaust,
high-performance dream machine.
That was me. All me.

Where I Come From

I come from never-sleeping rust,
    from an astrology of kicked-up dust.
From tantric turntables playing the soulphonic sounds
    of Motown lemme hear ya get down.
From rock and roll uranium 238
    which is made up of 92 protons of sweat,
    and 146 neutrons of turn it up to 10.

I come from a double back flip,
    from one of Cary Grant's acid trips.
From a Steve McQueen car chase
    and the Mona Lisa's face.

I come from you sleeping quietly in bed,
    from the X on Manson's forehead.
From the slow inhale of opium moments;
    opium moments winding through time,
    connecting to the places deep inside us,
    places deep inside us that say...

Every moment is a breath / Every breath is a word /
Every word is love / Every love is now /
Every now is everything...

I come from a dense lexicon of dog logic,
    from the gestalt of the Rock of Gibraltar,
from I like what you do
    but don't quit your day job.
I come from the smell of gasoline,
    the spark of first fire,
and a triple ohm choir. From three hits

of white crosses at a Kiss concert
circa the *Love Gun* tour.

I come from Are you sure we should be doing this?

From the Grim Reaper's belly button lint,
babbling Scrabble pieces, and an abracadabra thesis.
I come from the vibration of bells;
bells singing down into
the places deep inside us,
places deep inside us that say...

Every moment is a breath / Every breath is a word /
Every word is love / Every love is now /
Every now is everything...

I come from hummingbird beer burps,
from evening's first song in a cricket church.
From what part of NO do you not understand?

From Hey Joe where you goin' with that gun in your hand?

I come from absinthe kisses and Cadillac Ranch blisses.
From a knife in the chest to Stop You're Under Arrest!

I come from the language of honeybees,
from a bee's knees,
and if you please,

I come from a horse.

A horse in the blood that knows no fear;
a horse in the blood that gallops full on,
wild and wanting into those places deep inside us,

places deep inside us that say...

Every moment is a breath / Every breath is a word /
Every word is love / Every love is now /
Every now is everything...

Mistake

People often mistake me for skeletons in their closet.

For skeletons they
studied in 10th grade
biology.

For skeletons of operatic apoplexy

singing and flopping around

in the bing-bang-boom

of 3am blues.

People often mistake me for a low fog

rolling lazy over
Sunday morning
Georgia fields.

People often mistake me

for some kinda noise in their stomach.

The kinda noise

that could be played along

with hillbilly bop-
stomp Appalachian
jug music,

banjos shot fulla bullets,

harmonicas in heat,

looney-tune drunk-moon slide guitar
blues,

and somehow it would all fit. Somehow, it would all

just

make

sense.

People often mistake me for Jupiter aligning with Mars.

For the
Big
Bang.

For that distant pang in their hearts

clanging on and on for some love or loss.

Like a phone that won't stop ringing,

screaming like a check that bounced

or a bouncing baby

or a country
dog with
rabies.

People often mistake me for you. But you'll never mistake me for you.

And
that's
a
real shame.

'Cause sometimes I kinda wonder what it'd feel like to be you.

People often mistake me for that numb feeling

that rushes through them when they look in the rearview mirror

and

see

sirens.

Or when they're caught in a lie.

Or when they feel like the sky is falling

d
o
w
n

inside

of
them.

People often mistake me for their alarm clock first thing in the morning.

Or sex first thing in the morning.

Or a hangover first thing in the morning.

People often mistake me for all the mistakes they've ever made in their lives.

And let me tell you, that's a hard one to live

down.

That's
a hard
one
to
escape.

Especially when you're being introduced to some girl's father for the first time,

and she says:

"Daddy, I'd like to introduce you to all the mistakes you've ever made in your life...."

My Beautiful Suffering

Last night I drove on down,
down to Siren Town
    to the accident scene.

You were there, my suffering
looking as beautiful as when we first met;
    when I let you inside me, deride me.
Made my blood & bones your home,
believed you when you said
    you only needed a place to say for a few days.

But how things changed, deranged
and there you were, my beautiful suffering
last night down in Siren Town
    at the accident scene. Looking like
a dream bathed in moonlight
as you kneeled beside my chalk outline.

You wrapped me in a shroud of
my Scorpio star cloud,
turned your voice up loud, and said
that my eyes were windows
    I could jump out of time and again.

And the way you said my name,
like a big old punch in the face.
High-octane mean, gargling with gasoline.
Your smile a gunpowder sunflower
blowing me to pieces at the witching hour.

That's why I'm ready to get rid of you,

ship you off to Club Dread
    or better yet
have you suck some eternal sleep
from the shotgun barrel of death.

'Cause I'm tired of granting you immunity
from all my crimes.
    Yeah, I've done my time–
I've spent way too long
imitating the way your body speaks.

It's the shaking of plate tectonics,
the combined phonics of Mother Nature & destruction.
But that's how you've loved me, shoved me,
    couldn't get enough of me.

And even though I've eaten enough of your pills
to make my mind go satellite
it's all right. 'Cause right now
    I've got both feet on the ground.
Somewhere bells turn themselves inside out
to imitate this sound:
the sound of my voice, my breathing,
    me finally being alive.

Right now, my beautiful suffering
I don't need your help
in counting all the monkeys around me
to know evolution

ain't what it used to be.

But that's okay
'cause I can swing through the trees with the best of them,

the rest of them. I can devolve,
revolve around your fiery planets
out in deep, deep space—

the place where gravity has left me
and weightlessness is a beautiful, dark-eyed girl
named Maria.

How she caresses me,
blesses me with supernova novenas
light years from you, my beautiful suffering.

Your love hole's gone black hole,
your laser's gone razor.

Out in that deoxygenated dark
it ain't a lark the way you press against me
skin against skin,
sin against sin.

You know secrets I've never breathed to another soul.
You know my every blunder,
shadow me harder
than a social security number.

And while there were nights
I'd run my hands down your back
to read the bones of your spine
like a lovers' Braille

right now there ain't nothing you can do or say
to make me want you anymore.

Yeah, I'm closing that door,

drawing that line,
clearly defining the difference
    between risk & suicide.

Right now, my beautiful suffering
you do nothing to please. You ain't even
worth an atom of energy
    it takes to sneeze.

You & your soap opera dramatics, so tragic.

You reek so bad I gotta hold my nose
    'cause your mothball gossip's been
stinking up my clothes,
    making everything I eat
even the air I breathe
    taste as bad as combat-boot stew,
lousy as mail-order kung fu.

For so long, I didn't know what to do,
couldn't protect myself.

Was nothing but a magnet for machine guns & mace.
    Didn't have a trace of good karma, more like
the dharma of detritus; a phlebitis of
    mumbledom & doubletalk
granting me a dual master's degree in demonology
& dental floss.

For a while there
things were pretty black—

far more annoying than beach sand up my butt crack
and now it's all got me way past mad:

    the Jurassic spark to set off some murderous blast.

So let the Eternal Deejay
drop the needle down onto our whack-attack tracks
    as I try to relax.

'Cause what I've finally learned is that
when we the living sing
it's okay to be a bit off-key—
    our blood & bones can bear the dissonance.

Are you listening to me, my beautiful suffering?

'Cause right now I don't need to be
wall-to-wall Sodium Pentothal
to tell you the truth. And even though
    you may think it uncouth

you're nothing but the dagger that stabbed Caesar,
    puppy love gone geezer,
        a hookah jukebox run dry,
            superstition morticians,

a guitar that does nothing but cry.

Malarial tambourines ringing out the song
of sick-ass dynamite:
David Berkowitz, Mary Bell, the Schizophrenic Firesetter
all rolled up tight
    B'BAM!

A lifetime of Mondays & rain,
    a bullet in the brain, a bullet train
        barreling into a dead-end station,

a one-way conversation.

And right about now, my beautiful suffering,
I'm feeling sick & tired of talking to myself.

Down Across Girl

Boy parks car, puts arm around Girl.
With his free hand he changes stations, those radio stations.

Girl arches back, bends and blends her body
into those free-flowing airwaves.

Boy thinks, let me not disturb this dance; so
robbing gasoline from schemes, he instead sits quietly,
whispers Girl's name.

Girl sees heat lightning move through Boy
as she leans in
places her lips against his,
their mouths opening
tongues trading spit—the liquid equivalent of
truth, truth or dare, $e=mc^2$.

Outside car, he stands in shadows, waiting, listening to the muffled tones of radio. Spies the two lovers intertwined and remembers how in his own life, there's been something like this. Something like love: the whispered music of the knife sliding wistfully in and out of some woman's belly.

Inside car—
Boy thinks how, divided from Girl by city traffic and
summer heat,
it has been such a long way to fall
before reaching her kiss.

Girl laughs.
Her hair falls down around shoulders like

first handfuls of dirt thrown into the grave.
She opens her blouse; lets Boy touch her all over.
Says: "Tear me down with your switchblade mouth.
Interrogate everything that has been left sleeping in me.
Find it guilty. Sentence me
to death. Strap me
in your electric chair. Shock me,
make me feel alive."

Outside car, his teeth bite down. Teeth tear light. Tear light from moon. As blood rises in his mouth, he wonders whether it's this taste of blood or something more that has shown him the way to their door.

Inside car–
Boy's hands move down, down across Girl.
Down across belly, along thighs.
Boy's hands move like earth;
the earth that gives rise to flowers, to day and night.

Girl breathes in, out.
Makes herself as smooth as stone.
Makes herself a part of earth;
the earth that gives rise to flowers, to day and night.
Makes herself a part of earth–the earth where they belong.

Outside car, he blinks once, twice, as killing instinct races by at speed of light. Races through his heart: the devil's highway–the place where, with each beat, fires collide in overdrive. Fires that make hands shake; make trigger finger burn. Make trigger finger rise to test night air; the air that cools, makes voices call out. Voices telling night to wrap itself around his gun like a touch, a muzzle. For, if death should come to them, he thinks, it should come quietly, peacefully.

Inside car—
Boy's nomadic tongue
wanders across the undiscovered lands of Girl.
With every taste he goes back to the origins of man,
discovers fire, the wheel.

Girl hears crackle of static over radio.
Thinks it's a distant storm playing over the line. She hums,
lets her voice drop dizzily as if into a place
in green summer grass.
She tells Boy:

"I'll let you do anything."

Outside car, he takes aim, and says: "Let this lead rain down around your heads. Let it circle holy, leave halos of blood." And so there is the cry, the cry of gun. And so he feels the recoil. Feels the trace of powder burns like his lips; his burning lips across theirs. And kiss by recoiled kiss, he travels through their shattered bonework homeland. And kiss by recoiled kiss, the bell of bullet makes such a beautiful sound as it moves through them. And to this music, he sings his own words; words scrawled in lead, like the jagged, striated confessions held within his most personal diary.

Inside car—
Boy's last dying thought is of that kiss:
the kiss of Girl. And so his spirit
takes that kiss, rises into night,
beyond stars, moons, and planets
straining against lonely orbits.

While back in car—
wrapped in jewels of final breath,

Girl thinks of love. How unlike
whisky or wings, it was always the thing
that could ease her mind,
cure her soul's troubled gravity,
bring her back down to earth
so peacefully.

With her last bit of strength
Girl reaches for Boy, closes her eyes
and lets love,
like that bullet,
take its course.

She lets it lay her,
She lets it lay her down.

Bones

Sometimes I feel like I'm filled with bones—
    Bird bones
        Lullaby bones
bones sung heartbroken and moaning through some
    Hangover Radio bones
        Dust bones
            Shadow bones
                Alone bones.

When this happens
tell my mother I never meant to hurt her
I never meant to leave
it was only 'cause of these bones—
    Ghost bones
        Buchenwald bones
            Cancha Hear 'Em Moan bones?
                Rain bones
                    Whisky bones.

These bones are wanted in 14 states.
There're X-rays of me in post offices all across America.
These bones are my worst nightmare come true.
These bones have come home to roost. I can feel 'em
knocking against the doors of my flesh, but
I ain't gonna let 'em in.

'Cause I know these bones—

    Torture bones
        Starvation bones
            Tone-deaf bones.

Bones that break themselves,
herniate themselves, mistake themselves
for Armageddon, or

    Boredom bones, bones, bones.

Homeless bones
    Loveless bones
        Seconal bones
            Cemetery bones

LOUD BONES

    Atom Bomb bones
        Babylon bones.

One day soon
everything's gonna collapse,
cave in on itself, and these bones
are gonna be left lying in some Hollywood bar
in the middle of the day, telling lies,
and buying drinks for people

with money these bones don't even have.

'Cause these are
    Broke bones
        Bad Check bones
            Unwanted bones
like some door-to-door preaching
    Jehovah Witness bones.

You see,

this is what happens
when you meet your bones for the first time at some party
and everything's under lit and overdressed,
and you never end up getting what you really want
anything that's gonna last.

'Cause these are
    Blasphemous bones
        Tubercular bones
            Do Not Pass GO or
                Collect $200 bones.

Then there I'll be left lying in that Hollywood bar
in the middle of the day,
face-to-face with my own bones, saying:

"Hey, I think I've seen you somewhere before."

And these bones'll be saying:

"No, man. You must be mistaken.
I'm somebody else's bones."

And even though these bones'll be looking at me
eye-to-eye, heart-to-heart, toe-to-toe,

shin bone-to-shin bone,

still these bones'll be talking to me, telling me lies,
and buying me drinks

with money these bones don't even have.

Smoke and The Smell of Cheap Whisky

Forgive me, Lord. Last night, I cut a man while standing in the jukebox light over at The Circle Bar. There was that red and golden glow surrounding me as if I were blessed. So what if beyond that brightness were only broken things, smoke and the smell of cheap whisky? Inside that light, I could do no wrong.

That's how I was able to act so fast.

There was that guy coming at me with a broken bottle, you see. Didn't like the way I looked, I guess. Said he thought the color of my blood would look nicer on the outside. But my knife had wings, Lord. Two cuts, that's all it took.

Two cuts like the sign of the cross.

Carrie. She saw the whole thing. Was sitting at the bar drinking tequila. Had a head full of 80-proof Jesus and a honey creek running right through the middle of all her young rage. She followed me out of the bar and took me home with her.

Soon after, I was in her bed. It was like so many other beds I'd seen before: a place of love laced with morning glory and razor wire. Carrie pulled me down deeper into that bed. Outside her window there was a singing of blackbirds and faraway trains.

It was the closest thing to our angels.

Grow Wings or Cease to Be

Screams, lights, tattoo, lemonade, sixteen: she pulls at the rust-red lever of the amusement park ride. Muscles rise beneath her summer-beaten skin. She looks to the sky. Sees me in her ghostly roller coaster. I can feel the pressure of all things as I ascend. *Lemonade, sixteen, screams:* at the roller coaster's first drop, fear escapes me like a criminal at prison break. Whiplash, weightlessness. The boardwalk pulls out from beneath my feet. One last wish before the ground rushes back up to meet me—grow wings or cease to be. *Sixteen, lights, screams:* she says about her faded tattoo, it was for her first love, Fred. He taught her how to drive a stick, but turned out to be a real son-of-a-bitch. I tell her how the colors look so nice tonight. All the reds, yellows, blues and greens. How they flicker-flash. She laughs. Tells me I haven't seen enough. Says I'm still too young. *Tattoo, lemonade, sixteen:* she says that after Fred she needed a change. Likes working the roller coaster ride. Likes the feel of steel and people's lives in her hands. Makes her ache. Gives her strength at the end of the day. *Lights, screams, lemonade:* the taste of her kiss when she lets me in. Bitter. Sweet. Pulp between the teeth. She doesn't pull away. Calls me Baby Candy. Sweet in the mouth but gets stuck around the tongue. I tell her I sleep standing up. I am ready to run away with her. She pulls another lever. I drop fast. Reach for the ocean, its alphabet of sound. Rearrange the letters to say "I love you" a million different ways. *Screams, lights, tattoo, lemonade, sixteen. Screams:* I reach for her. *Lights:* again. *Tattoo:* she is there. She is not. She is there again. *Lemonade:* her kiss. Bittersweet. *Sixteen:* hold taste on tongue. *Screams, lights, tattoo, lemonade, sixteen:* fall again, this time harder, faster than before. Say "I love you" a million different ways. A look in her eyes like letting go, letting go of me, letting go of everything. The boardwalk pulls out from beneath my feet. One last wish before the ground rushes back up to meet me—

grow wings or cease to be.

All The Times

All the times I stuck something up my nose and couldn't get it out: 2.

All the times I said "Under Dog" instead of "Under God" when reciting the Pledge of Allegiance as a kid: 41; 15 by accident; 26 on purpose.

All the times I made prank phone calls to bowling alleys: 59; to bars: 68; to some random schmoe I picked from the phonebook: 197.

All the times I spoke in Pig Latin: ifty-fay ive-fay.

All the times I yelled for some band other than Lynyrd Skynyrd to play "Free Bird": 6.

All the times I regretted not wearing underwear for fear of suddenly dying in public: 31.

All the times I wore swim fins in public: 80; as a joke: 3; in all seriousness: 77.

All the times I received the Congressional Medal of Honor, the Nobel Peace Prize, or the James Beard Cooking Award: 0.

All the times I kissed someone of the opposite sex, including my mother: 13,601.

All the times I woke up in a strange bed and didn't know how I got there: 5.

All the times someone pointed a gun at me and threatened my life: 3.

All the times I took mushrooms: 7; acid: 4; smoked pot: 93.

All the times I witnessed dogs get locked up while having sex: 2.

All the times I accidentally witnessed my parents having sex: 2.

All the times I had dreams of losing hair: 84; losing teeth:

33; being naked in public: 42; being late for a test: 61; flying: 93.

All the times I lied to my parents: 3,018.

All the times I think they lied to me: 12,744.

All the times I was over-dressed for an occasion: 5. Underdressed: 79.

All the times I sold something door-to-door, Fuller Brush: 1; newspapers: 4; greeting cards: 6.

All the times I lost my car keys: 10; money: 33; drugs: I can't remember.

All the times I pulled off insect wings for no good reason other than curiosity, stupidity, or cruelty: 15.

All the times I cheated on a test: 23. On a girl: 2.

All the times I used God's name in vain: 358.

All the times he's used my name in vain: 0, I think.

All the times I murdered strangers in my thoughts: 541; loved ones: 6,567.

All the times I shoplifted: 8; got caught: 2.

All the times I stayed up all night just so that I could see the sunrise: 49.

All the times I bought a product that said I'd either get rich, gain confidence, find God, zap pimples, attract girls: 22,316.

All the times I wished I had more time: way, way too many times.

Because of Camp

Author's Note: The American Camp Association created a video in which actors and musicians share how their lives were changed for the better "because of camp." After watching their video, I realized that I'd had a very different summer camp experience...

Because of camp I developed my first severe case of poison oak.

Because of camp I discovered that rock climbing didn't build confidence, just bruises.

Because of camp my very first French kiss was with a circus arts girl whose tongue moved around in my mouth like a rabid skunk on roller skates.

Because of camp I thought that all girls French kissed that way, so I began kissing the same way too.

Because of camp hardly any girl ever wanted to kiss me. Only the crazy circus arts girl.

Because of camp I developed my first severe case of pink eye.

Because of camp I learned that I could lip-synch the hell outta "Stairway to Heaven."

Because of camp I discovered that I enjoyed lanyard making far more than instructional swimming and horseback riding combined.

Because of camp I learned that the foxy girls rarely went for the lanyard-making guys—especially the ones with pink eye, poison oak, and couldn't kiss for shit—no matter how badass they were at lip-synching "Stairway to Heaven."

Because of camp I discovered the true beauty of bouncing breasts during a volleyball game.

Because of camp I realized that I totally hated volleyball, but kept playing because of the breasts.

Because of camp I discovered that the girls in the dance program were far hotter, and far better kissers than the girls in the circus arts program, but that on first hook-up the circus arts girls would easily go to third base, while the dance girls would only go to first.

Because of camp I discovered that most kids, without any hesitation or sense of remorse, would gladly torture and kill any insect or woodland creature they could get their hands on.

Because of camp I learned that I totally sucked in both carpentry and martial arts.

Because of camp I never got a chance to score with the girls I found remotely interesting because they were either getting scammed on by the male counselors or the guys that excelled in carpentry and martial arts.

Because of camp I learned to see backwards and forwards at once because no one could be trusted; especially the animal killers, the male counselors, and the guys that excelled in carpentry and martial arts.

Because of camp I took numerous enrichment classes–drama, SAT prep, photography–and realized that I only excelled in one: crime science forensics.

Because of camp I learned that, yes, I could still be severely depressed, even in the great outdoors.

Because of camp I discovered that when you flip over in a canoe, once you hit that cold, dick-shrinking water and your balls go up into your throat, even your closest of friends suddenly adopt the mentality: *Every man for himself.*

Because of camp I learned to truly despise tie-dyeing. And balloon animals. And yo-yo tricks.

Because of camp I learned that I was prone to sleepwalking and snoring, but could make one hell of a Smores.

Because of camp I discovered that both golf and ceramics were a hell of a lot more tolerable after smoking a joint.

Because of camp I learned that the whole camp experience had very little to do with my parents wanting me to have an enjoyable summer, and more to do with them just wanting to get me out of their lives for a month.

Because of camp I learned in religious studies class that if my parents didn't accept Jesus Christ as their savior they'd go to hell, but that I wouldn't.

Because of camp I learned that that maybe wasn't such a bad idea: having my parents in hell while I kicked back in heaven.

Because of camp I discovered that the apocalypse didn't necessarily have to be all war, famine, and death. It could simply be having to attend golf or ceramics class without a sufficient buzz.

Because of camp I learned that the girl with Bells Palsy—which made half of her face go numb and uncontrollable—would actually turn out to be the prettiest girl there after a week's worth of antibiotics.

Because of camp I discovered beer pong. And consequently learned that what I lacked in ping-pong skills, I sufficiently made up for in drinking and barfing abilities.

Because of camp I learned that the kids on crutches always got the most attention. So during the night, when no one was around, I'd jump off the Smokey the Bear statue, trying to break my legs by landing on my knees. But it never worked:

I always landed on my feet.

Excommunication

The initial separation was the hardest thing:
the tearing away from flesh, bone, and old habits.

A corrosion of loss clotted in his still-unformed wings,
while somewhere in his ghostly remains of memory
lingered a woman's kiss–
sweet as gardenia.

He could remember that much,
remember that much of his life. He knew
there'd be things like this
he'd always remember. He knew he could
never die of forgetting.

As he rose
he twisted in the wind,
second-sight staggering behind
as he looked down to see the one he once was:

the one who now lay
by the side of that lonely desert road
heaped and foul in a pool of blood
with a voice answering only to carrion.

Right then, he wanted to erase his name,
turn himself inside out and experience
the morphine-serenity of dreamed-on clouds.

But all he could do was rise.

Brushing past birdsong and sun's roaming gold,

a pained smile came to his face. This lightness,
this gradual rising
was almost too much to bear.

Soon, however, he realized
there was no more fear of blood or time,

there was only the rising.

Again he sensed
that woman's kiss
lingering somewhere
in his ghostly remains of memory.

He knew
there'd be things like this
he'd always remember. He knew he could
never die of forgetting.

world without dogs

she had hands like jesus,
stigmata like a burning sun brilliant to the touch.

she said she could live in a world without dogs
and i thought that rather strange
seeing how i'd only asked her the time of day.

the radio lobo of loneliness
howled another song in my bones
as i held her like the suicide holds the knife.

she asked me to kiss the moon from her mouth,
to honor, then destroy her hesitation angels,
to speak the very dust and rust of her fallen empires;
to grow old with someone, something
that shares the same blood type as her sense of loss.

i fell down on my knees before her,
not so much out of honor
or some strange ceremonial code of conduct,

as it was because the satellites were flying low overhead that night.

because joan of arc was lighting fires in my mind,
teaching the stars how to fall out of the sky
in a million shattered pieces.

because something in the night
was speaking to me like writing
letters to the dead,

and i was feeling like my first words would be my last.

she fell down next to me, laughing,
giving me a necklace made of
river stones and her childhood.
as she smiled, silence and alibis
like strange ceremonial smoke
anointed her sleeping queen of grief.

i held her hands, her hands like jesus,
as the radio lobo of loneliness
cradled us softly over the wire

before everything simply disappeared.

Journey & Suffering

karma driving school

for J.L.

let's go back to the very beginning / get in that car / get behind the wheel / rev the engine to pure devotion / our each and every dream—sparkling motion / relearn brake, gas, clutch / not so much to speed us through these streets / but to clearly see / that our each and every action / ripens into results / bad equals bad / good equals good / it's not some tricky math / nothing like finding the perimeter of all human suffering / what it is, is the world coming from us / not at us / karma driving school

so get behind the wheel / upshift / downshift / buddha compassion / happiness and regret / cause and effect / oh road, be my teacher as I hurtle down highway / wrapped inside metal and machine dreams / moving faster than steve mcqueen / speeding between collisions of thoughts: anger, guilt, pity, passion / where the slightest stray of attention / a delay in stepping on brake or gas / can cause my next breath to be my last / shed that crash-addict skin / for the clear, wide-open highway of the here and now / karma driving school

so relearn brake, gas, clutch / not so much to get us from the eastside to the westside / but to let us hear those spirit wheels turning / burning sacred whisperings into road / transcendental transmissions / connecting me to you to everything between heaven and earth / total understanding / not some soul-sick lamentation trying to downgrade us to retrograde manifestation / and when we spin out of control / wondering whether our lives are crazy beautiful or simply tragic / turning heads like a car accident / it's time we stop starring in all those killing floor films / running through our minds / karma driving school

so uplift / downshift / all roads can lead us to eternal bliss / rev the engine to pure motion / our each and every dream—sparkling devotion / yet even with velocity as my bride / I know I can never outrun those distances / that sometimes lie between you and me / wondering how I ever got so far off course / from you and me / love lost / love gained / feel the pain / rubble, trouble / all the ashes from our past / the poisons and pleasures we breathe in / from all those fires we've set with our own hands / and when you and I collide and ignite / we glimpse those tiny lights inside each other's hearts / are they the signs of a new beginning / or everything dying before it even starts? / karma driving school

so make it real / get behind the wheel / drive it like you stole it / but deep down know you truly own it / so maintain presence / share the road / don't drive too fast or too slow / know that red lights lead to green lights / which can sometimes lead to thoughts becoming so misleading / believe in not believing / a once-beautiful song turned so down and out / kinda like phil spector's wall of sound come crashing down / bad equals bad / good equals good / it's not some tricky math / nothing like subtracting human avarice from elation / oh revelation / what it is, is the world coming from us not at us / karma driving school

so make it good / make it true / know that the same light that falls on me falls on you / know we're love and light everlasting / shraddha instead of blah-blah / this stop: soul-crushing samsara / with a possible transfer to beautiful nirvana / so relearn brake, gas, clutch / uplift / downshift / all roads can lead us to eternal bliss / and when you look in the rearview mirror / to see your fears sneaking up on you / like an unmarked police car / raging through slaughter / coming at you with everything but holy water / just remember we build our own ghosts / so we can destroy them, too / nothing is anything until we make it something / karma driving school

Crash

You and me
sometimes all we do is crash,
like when we drive
    or when we live and die or sleep—

when our night dreams and bodies become prisons of pain
so deranged, held captive by sickness and disease,
inertia and speed. That's when you and me
    we crash.

Crash as far away from the womb
as we've ever been in all our lives.

High up in that atmosphere of sadness
we're surrounded by all the things that make us bleed:

one part gravity, two parts uncertainty
and the last, regret—
that's the part that makes us fall back to earth
    like heaven undone,

crushed by the riot heat, mistaking ether for Eden,
calling upon St. Vicodin,
screaming we're in pain again,
    wondering whether we're a living sin,

praying to be put out of our misery,
maybe hit-and-run by that car
where Mr. Money's riding shotgun.

'Cause all we're asking for is a little bit of cash,

a little bit of flash, a little bit of
upward mobility, nobility.

Yeah, you and me
we're tired of crash-and-burning down
our bird-bone shrines
    to fleeting time.

Tired of fate making cruel constellations
out of all the scars
we've carried through our lives,
    dreaming on those body stars so maligned,
so overrated and depredated
when all we really wanna do is crash—
crash through our walls of pain,
    get to that place where the sky has no end,

and once again
we become the ethereal conjugation
of the verb breathe
    just breathe...

And I don't know if I ever told you or not
but many years ago I crashed real hard—
was on a rainy San Francisco day,
happened so fast
all the hairs on the speed-of-light's chin turned gray.
There was no one around to witness my passing;
in a flash
I was made ghost, gangrene, and grand mal everlasting.
And ever since that day
so much of my living has been done like a splinter,
a sickness,
or the loneliest of winters beneath your skin...

That's why sometimes I crash and blur,
find myself at a loss for words.
So forgive me if my exhalation's ever
    a flock of startled birds.
It's only 'cause I sometimes wonder
how this life's ever
    gonna work.
Especially these days with people getting crazy—
gets hard to tell the difference between
    John Wayne Gacy and a Macy's store clerk.

And when this crazy history's broken record
finally stops repeating itself,
then maybe we can begin to write a new song,
    one saved soul at a time.

But until that first line
    let our freak flags be unfurled, let us be
the shot heard round the world.
    A shot so loud it'll make us weep,
wake us from our cult of sleep.

That's when our outlook
will start getting clearer.
We'll stop being the things a dirty bomb sees
    when it looks in the mirror.

We'll become a million blisses,
peaceful uprisings coded into our kisses.

And all the regret,
all the dead we've buried
deep in the dirt beneath our fingernails,

well it's time to raise our hands to the sky,

let those restless spirits fly.

Let them be released with love and ease—
a conflagration congregation finally at peace.
'Cause all we're really looking for is to be
free of strain, free of pain,

get beyond that weight.

And before it's too late,
right here, right now
right beneath this mercy moon—
it's time for you to take the wheel,
do a little bit of driving
while I rest my eyes.

'Cause I trust you to get us closer to home
without crashing.

And when I say it's time, pull over,
relax, listen to the radio
while I take all our suffering and sadness
deep into the midnight desert,
strangle them with my own two hands
and leave them in a place
where only morning's buzzards
can find them.

Abilene Rising

The AM radio crackled and hissed
on account of the approaching thunderstorm.
Dark, heavy clouds
concealed the slow swirl of sunrise
along the far-reaching edges of Texas flatland.
For as far as he could see
and believe,
every little rock alongside road,
every blade of grass,
every trail of dust kicked up by wind
was a brief, beautiful thing
emanating from his heart—
as if he were the seed that had given birth
to such limitless exquisiteness.

Deep, ragged mantra of radio static
as he drove into head of storm.

Rain falling hard against car like Godspeak.

He: now bare-chested,
T-shirt wrapped tightly around wound,
blood-soaked, right hand still reflex-keen
gripping steering wheel,
driving down highway. He gritted teeth
from throbbing pain of bullet
lodged deep inside; hard burn somewhere near bone.
He rolled down window, stuck left arm out,
and let the blood that covered it flow away.

Let the blood be carried away

by all things so much greater than he.

He glanced in rearview mirror. Saw her
sprawled across backseat, silent now
as all sounds of her screaming and thrashing anguish
had stopped some half hour ago outside Lamesa.
Christ, he thought, even with a bullet in her gut
and barely holding on to life
she could still manage a striking pose.

That was one of the most intriguing things about her:
her poses.

He recalled the first night
he'd met her at the Circle Bar. How she
got him all lovesick and stupid in the knees
simply by just standing in the corner, drinking a beer.

She told him how she'd worked for a traveling circus
as a trick sharpshooter. Could knock the flame off
a candle at a hundred feet. After that,
she spent some time in Ann Arbor
learning the art of Zen Buddhism,
arm wrestling, and demolitions expertise
from some guy she met in a laundromat.
Said she'd come to L.A.
looking for a new way to apply her talents.

Then she pulled him close.

A faint smell of cotton candy and sawdust
rose from her body
like wild carnival spirits.

From that moment on, everything was a blur—
gunfast trigger-blue tattoo on air.

Now: a feeling of having woken from a bad dream.
The two of them, bullet-ridden bloody and
Abilene rising in the distance.

He didn't even think to take her seriously
when she'd said she wanted
to start robbing banks for a living.

But away they'd gone:
all the way from Venice, California
to Las Cruces, New Mexico—
leaving behind a trail of hundred dollar bills,
booze and blues.
Things had gone pretty well
until that botched convenience store job in Seminole
a few hours ago.

Never did see that one security guard
coming at them from the right.

She: screaming, falling.
He: draping her over his shoulder.
Guns blaring. Her blood
loping warmly, softly down his chest
as he ran for the car.

Guess it didn't really matter too much now, he realized.
He would've done anything for her. He would've
followed her anywhere.

He clicked off radio, rolled up window.

All quiet in the car
save for sounds of falling rain
and she in the back seat, breathing faintly;
body pulsing like some diamond in a dream.

Their breaths matched briefly between them.
Needed to find a hospital soon, he thought.

Christ, how could he even begin to explain all of this?
All this blood, all this money, all this love.

He reached back, brushed his hand along her cheek
then drew it back to his own face.

There was that same smell: cotton candy and sawdust.
The same smell that had attracted him to her
in the first place.

Christ, how could he even begin to explain all of this?
All this blood, all this money, all this love.

Hymn

From the wound is drawn the poison,
the forgotten moonlight that had been left for dead.

Body shudders in overwhelming struggle against darkness,
while somewhere in this blood
is the delirious midnight dance of hymns;
    the insight eyesight of spiritual height
    dreaming the star sign of highway prophecy.

And as the wheels turn
there is a little bit of God whispered into the road.
And as the wheels turn
there is a little bit of God whispered into the road.

Oh, I have ridden that Holy Ghost high
in search of the cloud you can cast your shadow across.

I have ridden that Holy Ghost
so that one day you may rise eternal and shining
like a new dawn incense,
    burning like blazing-angel silence,
    beautifying chaos,

making it hurdy-gurdy in the places
where we have all struggled without hope
for that moment of clarity.

In you, there will be constellations of prayer, and
meadow trance;
    the wildfire freedom of gravity in drag
out on the boulevard of saintly motion,

undressing ego to invisibility,
riding circus-winged and incandescent
into your Midwest breastbone to challenge the demons
that lie beyond your blur-beast blue door.

Oh, if ever in these days
you should find the need for me
to transform myself into cross or talisman
to put your mind at ease,

so be it.

If ever in these days
you should find the need for me
to transform myself into heaven dance
with resurrection hands
to lead you to your faith or bed of vision,

so be it.

If ever in these days
you should find a light behind your eyes
that will not go out,
that will not die,

no matter how far you have fallen
into an oblivion embrace
or another day doom,

do not be alarmed.

It is simply me,
waiting, wishing,
so wanting to show you the way

back to the nature of your own true home.

Pouring Down Silver

for L.F.

As he sat on his bed in that Vegas hotel room,
he took another swig of tequila, then pulled
a lock of her hair from his pocket. It was
the ribbon-tied lock of hair she'd given him
after they'd first said "I love you."
It was the lock of hair, soft and swirling
as the outline of her body at rest. It was
the lock of hair scented with loss, regret,
and unanswered questions.

It was the lock of hair, the lock of hair.

He slipped that lock of hair
down through the neck of the tequila bottle,
capped the opening with his thumb, and
shook the mixture. The hair changed
in length and form as it writhed
in its golden lair of liquid poison.
Like a mescal worm, it tempted him
to bite into it with all its
hallucinatory intrigue.

He prayed the lock of hair
would soon dissolve into the tequila. He prayed
that by the time he counted to ten
it would be gone, so he could
drink that woman down into the deepest,
darkest places inside
and be done with her.

Well past the count of ten, the lock of hair was still there.

He placed the tequila bottle on the nightstand,
wondering whether it would be he or that lock of hair
that would stay strong enough to survive.

Betting on his own survival,
he strained his ear against the whine
of the TV test pattern to listen
for the sound of his heart.
When that sound didn't come
he imagined his heart
already having turned into something
made of stone and silence. A stone and silence
like that of the highway—
the stone and silent highway
that had taken him from L.A. into Vegas that morning.

It was then he'd begun at the Stardust,
playing one slot machine over and over,
pulling at the mechanical arm
with all the fury his sorrow and anger would allow.

Around noon, the machine jammed up;
money spilling out non-stop. He stood there
mesmerized, staring at the machine
pouring down silver, quarters
falling to the floor, bouncing
brightly around his feet. He filled two buckets
with the twenty-five-cent pieces, then
ran out of the casino to hit
all the bars he could find.

Now, as he sat on his hotel bed
he again listened for the sound of his heart.

Just as he detected the briefest sign of life,
he heard an explosion. The blast
shook the room;
raped it, ravaged it,
tore it inside out a million times crying.

Wallpaper flew around in one great rush of tattered pieces.
The mirror broke into a fantastic, crashing opera
of catastrophic sound. Shards of glass
spun above his head in a brilliant array;
their precise glittering movements
reminding him of the showgirls
he'd seen at the Tropicana earlier that day.

As he reached out to touch the shimmering whirlwind,
a fireball shot through the wall behind his bed.
Suddenly, it felt like he had wings. He was flying
across the room. Flying like he had
in childhood sleeping dreams. He recalled
the tequila bottle on the nightstand
and wanted to go back for it.

But no matter how hard he tried to fly
against the annihilating waves of heat and energy,
he couldn't reach it. He'd already become
too much a part of the devastation–

his skin was melting off his bones,
his bones and heartbeat collapsing
into one magnificent whirl of ash,
his ashes mixing into the carpet,
the wind,
into the rest of Vegas
that was becoming one vast and brilliant heap of ruin.

A repeated series of blasts
tore his hotel room walls to rubble.

He wondered who was dropping all these bombs
and why, of all times, now?

There was another blast, and another.
Yet something was different:

the bombs were no longer exploding outside.
Now, he was being bombarded from within,
somewhere near his heart.

It was amazing, he thought, how the enemy
had not only devised a weapon that could work externally,
but internally as well.

He crawled across the floor,
grabbed the tequila bottle,
broke it against the nightstand.

Blood, tequila, broken glass: everywhere.

He couldn't tell where his own life ended
and the obliteration began.

Another round of blasts shook the room.
The third explosion in the series burst out his heart.

There were pieces of it everywhere—
shrapnel heart lodged in bones, burrowed in brain,
still other pieces shot wild into the night
and piercing the moon.

Everything around him grew smaller,
floating off in the enshrouding dark.

He held the lock of hair to his chest,
just over the place where his heart used to be.
The lock of hair
melted into that emptiness,
working like a morphine drip to ease his pain.

There was another blast. And another.

As his last memory-filled remains
were consumed by the next wave of devastation,
he realized he could still hear the whine
of the TV test pattern.

He found it strange that with everything around him gone
the set was still working. He wanted to turn it off
but couldn't quite reach.

Transition Into Turbulence

for Lisa Marie Nowak

"Lisa Marie Nowak is charged with the attempted murder of a woman she believed to be her rival for the affections of a fellow astronaut. Police officials say she drove 900 miles to Florida from Texas, wearing a diaper so she would not have to stop for rest breaks."—
New York Times, 2.07.07

Now some 600 miles into your trip,
you find yourself deep in the Florida panhandle–
Defuniak Springs, Bonifay, and Chipley.
All these towns and more
glow faintly in your rearview mirror
like tiny white dwarf stars.

And the early evening land surrounding you
breathes in and out. With every breath
the flat, forested land sends you messages.

On an inhale, you catch one. It tells you
to drive faster.

Because Orlando is still some 300 miles away
and you have to reach the airport in time
to catch that woman–
your rival, your kryptonite.

You step on the gas,
take the car up to eighty-five. As you
speed along, a cool wind
whips through your open window. The salt air
blows wisps of damaged hair across your eyes–
your wild and open eyes,

eyes burning like retrorockets,
eyes that have barely blinked twice since leaving Houston.

With those eyes
you stare straight ahead,
watch all the broken white highway lines
speed toward you.
Like shooting stars,
they are there for only a moment
then break apart and are gone;

only to create more brilliant stars
guiding you deeper into your strange orbit.

And while this transition into turbulence is a slow one,
it is an uneasy one.

There are your children back home:
your teenage son and his loud music, your little girls
and all their toys scattered across the floor.

You didn't know how to explain to them
your latest mission.

So you simply left them with a kiss
and some of your love.
Told them their mother
was going off on another one of her flights.

Thank God they can't see you now.

Their famous, timeless Space Age mom
now just some 43-year-old woman in a soiled diaper.

Turbulence.
That's what they'd think of your life right now:

turbulence.

You spin the radio dial
to drown out all the turbulence.

There's static,
country rock, classic and modern rock,
    more static.
Talk radio, commercials,
    still more static.
Bristling static. Static like all those
outer space stars and planets
    talking to one another static.

All the static makes you grip the steering wheel tight;
tight like love, unrequited love. And even though
you've died a thousand times in your mind
for that man who could never give you love, real love,
right now you die for no one.

Right now you only drive.

And the broken white stars go flying by.

As those stars speed by
you notice the open duffel bag
resting on the passenger seat.

It's filled with rubber tubing, plastic garbage bags,
latex gloves, a knife, and steel mallet.

You consider that mallet,
wonder what it will sound like
when it strikes your rival's flesh and bone.

Wonder how many strikes it will take that mallet
to maim, to kill that woman.

Ten, nine, eight...

With each blow
you break fingers,
shatter wrist bones,
as the screaming woman holds out her hands
to defend herself.

Seven, six, five...

As the mallet smashes into her skull
you hear a pop,
like that pop in your ears
as you make the transition into turbulence.

Four, three, two, one...

The woman crumples to the ground.
She is a puddle of moans and whimpers
as you smash her collarbone and ribs.

Zero...

Quiet now, her life
fades to space.
Deep black outer space.

Space.

With all these thoughts of murder and space
you think of God—
the bravest super astronaut of them all
floating holy out in the farthest reaches of the universe.

You wonder if there is truly a God
and, if so, whether he'll forgive you your sins;
wonder if he'll simply look the other way
as he washes the blood off your hands.

Surely he'll understand, you reason,
how difficult it can be
when you're merely mortal
and torn from your home,
thrust skyward against gravity's grip,
hurtled through cloud ceiling and dense waves
of satellite speak,

until somewhere in weightless orbit
you're left looking down,
witnessing the earth for what it truly is:

a huge, sleeping ball of beautiful blue
floating lonely in the dark
with no strings attached to any heaven
or securely guiding principles.

And the moon and distant galaxies
are no longer pictures in a book,
but are so tangible and reachable
and suddenly seem to make much more sense

than your own life.

So that when you burn through reentry
at hypersonic speed
in your fall back home,
where all your family and friends,
no matter how much
you adore them,
never quite revolve around the planet of you
the same way anymore.

And gravity.

All it does these days is pull you down,
down to this moment, right now:

You spot a sign for Orlando–
less than 200 miles away.

You check your watch:
t-minus killing time and counting.

Again, the night land surrounding you
breathes in and out, sends more messages.
On an inhale, you catch one. It tells you
to drive faster.

You take the car up to ninety.

And the broken white stars go flying by.

8th & Agony
for D.H.

It was at 8th & Agony—
there was blood in the streets
and someone screaming out:

"I am sorry, I am sorry for everything."

Or maybe it was Kansas—
the two of us driving down the highway;
everything was rolling and green,
and we were surrounded by hunger
and the hiss of electricity.

Or maybe it was San Francisco—
the rain coming down like words in a suicide note
and you, standing there
speaking the name of a woman;
a woman who scatters shadows like birds
as she descends from the sky with a kiss.

No, wait.
It was the telephone.
That's it, a telephone...

There was a night—
a night without stars. It could've been
the coffin already come, it could've been
some hallelujah dog gone hungry. Or maybe it was
thunder, beaten down and crying for the moon.

Or maybe it was that girl in a short skirt—
Sunset Strip, Friday night, looking for speed

and free drinks. It could've been the way
you told her with your eyes
that you had nothing for her, nothing at all.

No, wait.
It was the telephone.
It was me picking up that telephone to make a call...

It could've been me, it could've been
you gone ghost;
betrayed by the machine of desire,
desires burning, turning
like those wheels in the middle of Bad America–

the place where dreams lose their virginity
before they even know the alphabet,
before they even have time to say:

"Give me a chance to think about this. Give me time
to take this all in."

No, wait.
It was the telephone.
It was me picking up that telephone to make a call.
The telephone was ringing...

Or maybe it was the singing–
like that East Hollywood heroin in a red dress,
mainlining you with her rabid orgasms
and sex-beat circus.
Or maybe it was the magnet of pain
that brought us together in the first place.

And before this night is over

it could end so violently, or not.

Not go out on a bullet, but a nod—
the John Doe of Nods
toe-tagged at the morgue of melancholy;
unknown, alone.

No, wait.
It was the telephone.
The telephone was ringing.

There was the sound of a voice: Hello?
It was my voice.
Because it was you who was calling me,
calling me to say...

It could've been the crying. It could've been the dying.

It could've been that old woman on a Greyhound bus—
Sunday Morning, New Mexico—
waking you from sleep
with her talk of Jesus coming back as an Indian
living on some holy-headed reservation.

Or maybe it was the two of us turning into dust and leaves,
drifting away every time we speak.

And every day
I try to read the newspapers,
smoke signals,
the tarot,
tea leaves,
billboards,
the shudder of horses

to know who, what or where we are.

No, wait.
It was the telephone.
It was me picking up that telephone to make a call.
Hello?
It was the sound of my voice.
Because it was you who was calling me
to say goodbye for the last time.

Okay, for the last time, there was a telephone.
It was ringing.
It was: Hello?
Because it was you who was calling me to say goodbye for the last...

Okay for the last time there was a telephone.
It was me picking up that: Hello?
Okay for the last time...

It was you who was calling me to say goodbye for the last time.
It was you who was calling me to say goodbye for the last time.
It was you who was calling me to say goodbye for the last time.

When Words Meant to be Spoken Are Bottled Up For Too Long

When words meant to be spoken are bottled up for too long, those words stop showering and shaving. Crank speed metal at four a.m. Carve lines into your forehead with rusty knives. Illegally park in handicapped spaces, create fake ads on Craigslist. Those bottled-up words trade up for down, left for right, dropkick you into the shacklebone zone. They smile in public, beat you in private. Fill your mouth with rains and hurricanes, pee a circle around your soul and mark it for extinction.

When words meant to be spoken are bottled up, they make rotgut wine, start lying about their age, slap a bumper sticker across your ass proclaiming: *Graduate of the 12-Step Program for Underachievers.* Those bottled-up words French kiss barrels of loaded guns. Become chalk outlines on the streets of reason. Leave you stripped and abandoned like a stolen car. Rewrite your life in third person blank-eyed verse. They smoke too much, tip too little, forget the city of their birth. Collect countless coroner's reports and mold them into your shadow, then nail it to your feet.

Bottled-up words hog the sheets when you're trying to sleep. Babble static. Drop bombs of chronic confusion. Grind your teeth into tombstones, scribble obits into your every breath. They desecrate instead of elevate. Tie your thoughts in a noose, hang common sense at high noon.

When words meant to be spoken are bottled up for too long, they stamp your life: *Return to Sender.* Trash talk you from heel to horizon, yet always speak your name and credit card number loud and clear when checking into death's hotel.

See How We Are

How we live as freedom fighters,
easy riders,
bookworms and barflies.
The broken and abandoned.
Life takers, halo makers,
earth shakers, gravity breakers.

See how
we live everyday,
born and reborn into castes
of cruelty and consciousness.
Wild-eyed dreamers,
sucker-punched underachievers.

Wealth,
poverty, sickness.
Quick to wound,
slow to heal.
Each of us
part of the color wheel of pain:
bruises changing from purple to black,
to yellow and brown,
then to nothing at all.

We are.

Born and reborn
into ticket takers, record breakers.
Get ahead, fall behind.
Pushing and shoving
our way into

brawls, malls,
heart attacks,
and padded walls.

Face the strange.
Face the music.
Face the way
our lives are so
playable, pausable,
fastforwardable,
reversible.

We are.

Born and reborn
into crack, cocaine,
ecstasy, LSD—
haze and hallucinogens for daze.
Still the mushroom cloud
is the biggest mindfuck
of them all.

Spit, kick, punch our way outta the fray.
Suck, screw, buy our way back in.

We are.

Amnesia,
anarchy, accomplishment.
Love, hate, shame, blame.
Messiahs made
and broken faster
than changes in the
Stock Exchange.

Uptick, downtick.
Camera flash, muzzle flash.
The firing of brain cells,
and friendly fire.

It's all enough
to get us down,
shoot us up.

Syringes
filled with
TV, porn, gossip magazines—
temporary blurs and blisses
to charm us into submission
long enough
to slip the noose around our necks.

Hang 'em high, hang 'em low.
Any way the wind blows.

We are.

All a part of the emotional weather:
sunny with a chance
of clarity and conviction,
or cloudy with a 95% chance of denial.

See how we
downsize, sabotage, surrender.
Slaves to masters of detox and whitewash.
One brain hemisphere
stuck in the stone age,
the other catapulted
into the electronic age.

We're
radioactive, hyperactive,
reactive, stupefactive.
Digitally, genetically,
anatomically modified.
Annotated, ameliorated,
bifurcated, degraded,
underrated.

Eradicated.

Chant, pray, meditate
our way outta the maze.
Steal, kill, lie our way back in.

We are.

Born and reborn
into extermination camps,
slave labor,
and racism.
Compassion and equality
go without consensus,
while bombs keep getting smarter,
and violence becomes
the universally accepted
one size fits all.

See how
it's so hard
to relate, communicate.
Airwaves
filled with

endless oscillations
of
aggravations,
testifications,
and disinformation.

Doing our best
to break through
environmental noise,
cultural noise.
Physical,
psychological,
attitudinal barriers.
Ambiguity
of words and phrases—
a cacophony
of oxymoronic harmonics.

Say *what*?
Can you hear me?

We are.

Born and reborn
into personal invention, reinvention:
facelifts, new religions and belief systems.
So many comings and goings,
doings and undoings
that we often miss
our truest, highest selves
on the rebound.

Curse, condemn,
protest our way outta the malaise.

Bribe, jive, connive our way back in.

We are.

Lifesavers, deal breakers.
Healers, death dealers.
See how we
save the whales,
save the seals,
save the children,
while others
continually devalue,
mismanage and underfund:
health, welfare, education.
Corporations supersizing
while making
not-at-all happy meals
of the common man.

Bite into that one
and tell me if you feel any heartburn.

We are.

We were.

Born and reborn
from water, clay;
the tremblings of fossilized bones
turned word.
Through time,
our tongues soaked in rhyme, reason,
treason and malfeasance.

The seed of us taking root,
spreading across
wide-open spaces.
See how
we've flowered;
faltered;
gotten stuck
in cubicles, crisis,
and traffic.

See how we praise
courage and confidence.
Mayhem and doomsday angels.
See how we make our lives
a miracle, a mess.
A reliquary, an obituary.

Born and reborn
into power and imprisonment;
liberation, victimization;
travesties, savageries;
devotions and deities.

We are.

We were.

We continue to be:

The land of need and home of the underpaid.
The land of greed and home of the enslaved.
The land of the freed and home of the engaged.
The land of the unseen and home of the enraged.

Destiny & Enlightenment

The Los Angeles Book of the Dead
Words to be recited at the time of someone's death in this city...

O' Son and Daughter of Noble Birth,
now the time has come for you to seek a path.
As your breath stops, visions will appear.
And while on this journey from life into death,
if you should find yourself calling out:

"Oh Lord of Great Compassion,
am I beautiful enough?
Am I wearing the right clothes?
Do I have the right connections to get me into
where I'm going?"

To these concerns I say do not worry.

Release your fears
for soon you will find experience
to be the greatest teacher and healer.

And while there will be those of you
who find yourselves floating holy in
Beverly Center Buddha-realm beauty,
know that there will be others
left shuddering cold turkey in a
metaphysical Macarthur Park,
strung out on doubt as you try to
re-enter your own body
or the body of another
again and again.

Please understand this is not an option.
This is the type of suffering that must be endured.

There is no body that can help you now.

O' Son and Daughter of Noble Birth,
if you've done wrong
you can't go trading up karma like baseball cards,
thinking you'll end up with that prized
Tommy Lasorda 1988 Dodgers World Series winner.

So if you've lied, cheated, looted,
committed a drive-by shooting,
screwed your best friend's girlfriend / boyfriend,
left your cell phone on during a yoga class or movie,
now is the time your conscience is collecting
those sins and numbering them
on the bones of a South L.A. body count.

Yet if you should find yourself
in a La Brea tar pit hell
filled with dinosaurs, saber tooth tigers,
space aliens, and earthquakes–

don't worry.

Know that it's merely being created
by the special effects experts at Universal Studios
to ensure your journey
is the most exciting ride possible.

O' Son and Daughter of Noble Birth,
as you move through these afterlife streets
you will encounter many dreams and dead ends–

at the blink of a camera eye
you can sell a script for a million

or lose your soul like Faulkner in Hollywood.
With a name change and jeweled turban
you can reinvent yourself like Korla Pandit,
or have your own life taken
by any Manson, Menendez or Night Stalker.

Demons and protective spirits will take many forms–

there'll be moon-eyed Sirens of Overnight Success
singing fleeting love songs with
Carmen Miranda and Angelyne
in three-part harmony.

There'll be mandala-faced day laborers
with bent backs and calloused hands,
standing at freeway off-ramps, shouting:
"Espiritu d'azucar."
    Sugar spirit...
"Dáme tus besos de sangre dulce."
    Give me your sweet blood kisses...

O' Son and Daughter of Noble Birth,
in this cross-town journey
as you approach the eternally glittering womb
of the 101,
please keep an open mind as you meditate
on the connections you need to make
to ensure your safe passage to that area of the city
where you would most like to be reborn:

If it's the Valley–
    know that it has the tempting allure of Krispy Kreme
    and the porn industry,
    but otherwise, it's bland, flat,

has way too many mini-malls,
and looks like the worst parts of New Jersey.

If it's the Westside–
know that Venice has beats, hippies,
love-in drunken frenzies, and
Mother Ocean's deep embrace,
but the rents are incredibly expensive, and
Santa Monica's 3rd Street Promenade
is really Dante's Inferno.

If it's Beverly Hills–
know there's plenty of room at the Hotel California,
but you could still end up living in a mansion
with a Guatemalan housekeeper named Lucia,
whom you'll trust to raise your children,
but will still only pay minimum wage.

If it's West Hollywood–
know there are buff, beautiful fags and drag queens,
but restricted parking
for those with more than six percent body fat.

If it's Hollywood–
know the hills are still filled with
the rebellious spirit of James Dean and Timothy Leary,
while down on the boulevard
they've Disneyfied to stay alive.

If it's Koreatown or Hancock Park–
know there are rejuvenating spas,
palatial estates, and lovely Larchmont Village,
but you could still
end up being reincarnated as a dumpster

behind Chicken Day restaurant on Western.
And, well, that would pretty much suck.

If it's Silverlake–
know there are hip artists and rock bands,
but the prices are skyrocketing,
and the Cuban coffee is getting squeezed out
on account of the invading Westsiders
proclaiming themselves reborn-again Eastsiders.

Finally,
if you should decide
to be reborn anywhere near the Rampart District,
know that even after all these years,
even with all the negative press and attention,
a renegade police officer
could *still* decide to kill you
without the slightest provocation;
and that action alone
could have you being reborn out in the Valley
whether you like it or not.

And if after all this
you still have your doubts about where to reside
in this afterlife L.A.,
know that as Lord Stravinsky once said:

"The only way to escape L.A. is to *be* in L.A."

O' Son and Daughter of Noble Birth,
what you are ultimately looking for
is that place and position in this city
where you can feel omnipotent.

So before your last-breath checkout
be sure to check out your heart's true calling.

If it's singing across party lines,
breaking hypes and stereotypes
    that's fine.
You can be a non-rapping Caucasian in Leimert Park,
    a non-burrito eating African American in East L.A.,
        a non-housecleaning Chicano in the Palisades.

But if somewhere along your spiritual journey
you consult your Google Maps
to find that maybe you missed
    your last exit to Status Town,
don't let it get you down.

'Cause more than any Malibu beach house
you need to set your sights
on that transference to pure space—
the place where you can feel

total release.

And even though you're tired from your many journeys
you must still find the energy
to transform yourself into
an Echo Park Lake lotus flower
that can be offered to the Buddha of Complete Joy.

For this is the Buddha
that will keep you moving toward the lights:

the spotlights slashing your afterlife skies.

These are the lights calling you to the greatest premiere of all–
the eternal party
where you are the star,
where you are walking down the red carpet,
where you are smiling and waving to the cameras,

and we as your adoring friends and fans
can't help but hang on to your every word,
your every action,
wondering what you will say,

and where you will go next.

I Wait For You

For those born with a radarless heart, destined to wander in worried circles while others walk a truer, straighter path, I wait for you. Guide you.

For those who brave the sun, brave the deoxygenated black-hole dark to write epic poems in the vast spaces between glittering stars, I wait for you. Collaborate with you.

For those always ending up last in the soul's inner-beauty pageant, I wait for you. Crown you.

For those who voted Nihilistic and got their President of Nothingness, I wait for you. Dream a better world for you.

Gather fractured raptures, make whole, make one.

For those who've had all the wars of the world written into the lines around their eyes, I wait for you. Bear that history with you.

For those whose lives have been relegated to the B-side of that number one with a bullet hit called "My Gunned Down Life," I wait for you. Write a better song for you.

For those who work the graveyard shift in the morgue of loneliness, I wait for you. Work side by side with you.

For those fatal optimists, hope flourishing but cyanide on standby, I wait for you. Offer a taste of faith to you.

Gather fractured raptures, make whole, make one.

For those with atom bombs and ghost towns encoded into their DNA so that everywhere they go shit just keeps blowing up and no one ever stays around for very long, I wait for you. Rebuild for you.

For those who've shipped their lives off to fictitious addresses hoping to elude reality once and for all, I wait for you. Pick up that mail for you.

For those who've long since pulled the plug on their personal freak machines, I wait for you. Funky chicken, krump and downrock with you.

For those who speak from the heart, even when it is broken, knowing that cracked words are better than no words at all, I wait for you. Honor you.

Gather fractured raptures, make whole, make one.

A Dedication

This one goes out to all the hard-luck insomniacs whose mattresses are filled with a month of Mondays. This one goes out to the Lost Generation, the Beat Generation, Generation X, Y & Z. This one goes out to those whose spines are lightning rods. No wonder the blazing, brilliant light follows you wherever you go. This one goes out to Generation Elation, Generation Elevation, Generation Regeneration. This one goes out to those who can scrape the old, crippling stories from their bones. Make themselves Tabula Rasa. Blank slate. Brand new day. Anything & everything is possible. This one goes out to all the dogwalkers, streetwalkers, freedom riders & freedom marchers. This one goes out to those who are far from homogenous. More like slipslide, electraglide Superfly symphonic. This one goes out to all the teachers, healers, street sweepers & unity-minded leaders. This one goes out to our diseased world, our needing world. Our over-stimulated & under-educated world. This one goes out to those who give voice to the sky, to shy birds & sunshine. Those who sing out loud & proud, like they're on fire: new day's Creation Choir. This one goes out to our bleeding world, our well-meaning world. Our treasonous, peace & reason world. This one goes out to those who are the penicillin for whatever ails humanity. To the nurses in the 24-hour hospital of the troubled soul, constantly having to give desolation piss tests for faith. This one goes out to all the idiosyncratic angels that can only fly backwards, but still know how to pray it forward. This one goes out to those who understand that gravity is a condition we must sometimes fight against when wanting to commune with the lighter gods. This one goes out to our defiant world, our triumphant world. Our spastic, super-elastic, locked & loaded, fully automated world. This one goes out to those who thrive and are truly alive in the Universe of We. Those who are the flame. The pulsing blue star. Combustible angels. Morning's first light speaks your name. Your luminous version of ecstasy is etched into my flesh. This one goes out to our awesome world, Godawful world. Our sexting, vexing, foreclosed & bulldozed world. This one goes out to Our Lady of Collateral Damage, Our Lady of Ignorance & Greed, Our Lady of Automatic Weapons in the Hands of Murder-Lusting Thugs Let Loose on the Streets. Know that I pray for all you Ladies, and hope that one day soon you'll change your ways. Lastly, this one goes out to each & every one of you. All my scars—emotional and physical—have always had an ear for song. No wonder my wounds, and all my healings are so easily drawn to the music within you.

Certain Things About Certain Women I've Known

Anna was a metaphysical meteorologist. Could always predict whenever my heart's weather was nearing rain.

Jen was born under the sign of an electric guitar. She'd turn me up. Turn me on. Did anything but turn me down.

Doris took everything that wasn't nailed to the floor or superglued to my conscience.

Kelly would cage me. Let me roam wild in her heavy-petting zoo.

Fiona was my judge, jury and executioner. She never inflicted a painful death; more like the death of all my pain.

Certain things about certain women I've known...

Ashley was a blizzard in a box.

Heidi was a socially conscious super-ninja activist; an eco-friendly beauty, jamming crowbars into the phantom gears of hatred, ignorance & greed.

Justine's skin was brushed clean by the winds of myth. Her love was clear, true & fearless.

As for Dara: everything about her glittered. Even her smallest of afterthoughts: mother of pearl.

Victoria had a brain sharp as the devil's toothpick.

Allison had a libido like a busted-up piano. Any key you hit, nothing happened.

Certain things about certain women I've known...

Desiree was the antidote to gravity.

Alicia preferred specificity over brevity. If I were a shrink, I would've diagnosed her manic confessive.

Jaida subsisted only on a diet of rainwater & fairy tales. She eventually lost herself to the skies; became a lyrical, ever-changing cloud.

Gloria was a gothic nihilist. Dark as crow omen, death & destruction were her mother tongue.

Alexia was lovely as a Monet lily.

Debra was heroin and a slow train to Paris.

Certain things about certain women I've known...

Julie was a loaded gun in the house of faith.

Kadence was crazy as Armageddon off its meds.

Caitlin's heart could flood with such feelings that no ark, no matter the size, could save all the wild animal emotions trapped inside her.

With Saturn for a third eye, Esther's perceptions were heaven-sent. She was the Big Bang in reverse: the entirety of the universe gathered itself like a small child into the womb of her every word.

Just below Angela's lips was a door marked Eternity. "Kiss me," she'd say, "Then let's fall into forever."

If I Were a Bond Girl

If I were a Bond girl
I'd be *Thunderball* beautiful,
have a body like a smart bomb,
be Jill St. John, Britt Ekland and Barbara Bach
all rolled into one.

If I were a Bond girl
I'd be a geologist, a professor of Danish at Oxford,
a fully trained astronaut working for the CIA,
run my own flying circus, be a Japanese shell diver, an expert pickpocket,
or simply go by the code name XXX.

If I were a Bond girl
I'd be Ursula Andress emerging from the sea in a bikini,
have a heavily guarded island filled with women,
be able to make love in scuba gear, while orbiting the earth,
or in some remote location covered in diamonds.

If I were a Bond girl
I'd know judo, karate,
be able to crush victims to death with my thighs,
wield a crossbow, be a KGB assassin,
or decide to not live and die by the gun,
but to exact my revenge in bed instead.

Last week I went to visit a psychic,
asked if I'd ever been a Bond girl in a past life
or had the chance of being one in the future.
The psychic said:

"Gimme my fifty bucks before I answer your question."

After I handed over the cash
all she said was:

"Fat Chance."

If I were a Bond girl
I'd be headstrong and resourceful,
athletic and intelligent.
I'd be a complex villain or adventurous spirit
with a name like Dr. Molly Warmflash, Pussy Galore,
Kissy Suzuki, or Honey Rider.

If I were a Bond girl
I'd have the innate ability
to easily exchange the fatal nerve gas Delta 9
for a harmless sleep agent,
or go from battling villains aboard a space station
to decommissioning a nuclear weapons facility in
Kazakhstan
without breaking a sweat.

And though there may be times
when I'd be easily seduced by
a bottle of chilled Bollinger and a rose,
I'd still kick ass before the end credits rolled.

If I were a Bond girl
the best thing of all would be
that when things got rough, I mean *really* rough,
I'd somehow manage to steal a quick time out
for a few relaxing minutes in a hot tub.

It's gonna happen.
I don't care what anyone says.
I'm gonna be Grace Jones, Halle Berry, and Money Penny
all rolled into one.
What was I thinking anyway?

Bond girls don't go to psychics.

On Becoming An Urban Legend

Becoming an urban legend is simple.

When you want to become an urban legend you start out by sitting at home, alone, on a Friday night, doing your best to not think about all your friends out roaming the city—clubbing; drugging; strolling through art galleries featuring earth-tone paintings or famous sports photographs such as Mary Lou Retton in the 1984 Olympics—friends laughing, learning, while you, the still-not-yet-an-urban-legend, sit at home, alone, on a Friday night, feeling like a bottom feeder down at the dark depths of the popularity food chain, reading a book you've already read five times, doing your best to not think about all those friends out having a much better time than you, as you change out of your clothes, wash your face, brush your teeth, dig a Q-tip through your ear, recalling the countless occasions when parents, priests, doctors, teachers, all of them telling you it's not a good idea to stick a Q-tip too far in your ear because it could burst your ear drum or any number of other Godawful health risks; but there you are alone on a Friday night—still not yet an urban legend—digging a Q-tip, which is not really an official Q-tip Q-tip, but more like some flimsy, generic cotton swab you bought at the 99 Cent Store to save a few cents; digging it in your ear, realizing this generic-cotton-swab-in-the-ear feeling is the closest thing you're going to get to any excitement on a Friday night, and you relish in this generic-cotton-swab-in-the-ear feeling until suddenly it changes; becomes a harsh cocktail-straw-in-the-ear feeling, and now you realize you're not hearing so well out of that ear anymore, like everything's underground, underwater; and when you pull the generic swab from your ear you see the cotton end is no longer there, but now stuck in your ear;

and not thinking clearly you stick a finger in to dig it out, but that only pushes the cotton further into your ear canal; so you grab a pair of tweezers to dig it out, but you can't turn your head around far enough—definitely not like Linda Blair in *The Exorcist*—to examine your inner-ear in the bathroom mirror, so you drop the tweezers, run through your apartment, jump up and down, tilt your head, praying the cotton swab will simply dislodge from your ear, fall to earth like an object from one of Newton's gravity experiments, but when it doesn't happen you pick up the phone, and start calling friends; but not all your friends, only the one or two really close ones that won't laugh their asses off when they hear what's happened; but when you call those friends, all you get are their answering machines because it's a Friday night and, of course, they're out engaging in much more productive, provocative activities than sitting at home, alone, getting generic cotton swabs stuck in their ears; and as crazy as it seems you now realize you're going to have to drive yourself to the emergency room to get this little piece of cotton removed from your ear; so you put your clothes back on, jump in your car, get on the freeway, as you watch all the cars around you, how their headlights, tail lights float ecstatically through the ether of Friday night let's-get-it-on electricity, while you—the still-not-yet-an-urban-legend—drive yourself to the hospital; and when you get there, when you tell the white-smocked attendant why you're there, she gives you a look: the look that says I hope this isn't how you spend all your Friday nights, the look that says I want to laugh at you, pity you, spit on you for being here at almost midnight with a generic cotton swab stuck in your ear when there are much more serious cases like gunshot wounds, stabbings, car accidents for me to deal with; then the white-smocked attendant has you take a seat until another white-smocked attendant comes for you—some guy looking like

David Bowie, except if David Bowie were a short, well-tanned, bottle-blonde Filipino with a slight limp; and so you go with this different David Bowie, dreaming of Diamond Dogs and Scary Monsters as you follow him down winding, snaking, fluorescent-lit corridors as Code Blues and other commands crackle through the intercom; and when you get into the bowels of the emergency room where there are doctors and nurses all rushing around, treating patients in flimsy blue curtained-off rooms, the short, well-tanned, bottle-blonde Filipino David Bowie with a slight limp puts you into your own blue-curtained room—barely gives you a second look because to him you're just another patient, still-not-yet-an-urban-legend—as he says matter-of-factly that a doctor will be with you soon; and when he leaves, you touch the flimsy blue curtains surrounding you, and realize that that's the only thing separating *you* from the more seriously injured; that the line between life and death is really quite fine, fine as those flimsy blue curtains surrounding you, and just as you're about to pull those curtains open, cross over to the other side, that's when the doctor and nurse arrive; and when you tell them why you're there, the nurse responds: "You know I've only heard of this happening before, but I've never actually witnessed it, and now here you are, some guy with a Q-tip stuck in his ear, you're like one of those urban legends, wow, this is great"; and when the nurse says those words, you realize they're the words you've been waiting to hear your whole life, the words that no longer make you feel like a bottom feeder down at the dark depths of the popularity food chain; instead those words leave you exalted, raised to new glorious heights as you enter into the pantheon of urban legends; right up there with Altoids as sexual aids, attack of the camel spiders, gerbils in Richard Gere's butt; and before you can think of another urban legend you now accompany, the doctor has already grabbed a pair of tweezers, plucked the cotton from your ear, and has said: "There, done, you can go home now"; and you sit there stunned, almost wishing there had been more drama, like putting you under the microscope, under anesthesia, into stirrups, into surgery; anything but sitting in your flimsy blue curtained-off room, the doctor showing you the tiny piece of cotton that may as well have been a bullet in your head for all the pain and fear it had drawn up in you; but relax it's okay because you're an urban legend now, right up there with junior-high sex bracelets, the eye of God Helix Nebula, Mr. Rogers as a marine sniper/Navy Seal; and so you bolt out of the hospital, jump into your car, head back toward home, floating above the ethereal swirl of Friday night let's-get-it-on electricity; you take your car up to ninety, the engine screams louder than murder, louder than great sex as you rocket past all your friends and other partiers, insomniacs, and romantics; go ahead, drive faster, take your car up to a hundred, show everyone around you that you're much wilder, much crazier than the rest of the restless souls in this city; show them you're a force to be reckoned with; right up there with Hogzilla, the Hairy Hitchhiker, cyanide-laced deposit envelopes; go ahead, it's okay, you can do anything, you're invincible, you'll live forever in people's imaginations, be the story that's passed back and forth over the Internet, the office water cooler, over after-work cocktails; go ahead, live it, breathe it, be it, say it:

you're an urban legend now.

Find Them All And They'll Say

for Bukowski

Find the angry dog,
the dying houseplant,
the noncommittal monosyllabic babbling idiots
having a tailgate party in your first chakra.

Find the vice-president of the finger painting club,
the night clerk at the home for the terminally confused,
the 50-pound bag of fertilizer used for the garden
instead of a bomb.

Find St. Jude, Hey Jude,
the man with pentagram hands,
the woman whose kisses are weapons of bliss,
the black cat crossing your path,
the heart attack and scoliosis'd back,
the dogeared Bible and virulent virus,
the Band-Aid big enough for a fucked-up life.

Find, find, find them all and they'll say...

Find the strangled alarm clock,
the soul's X-ray machine,
the songbird with laryngitis,
the rosebud with a bellyache,
the chicken that shot himself by the side of the road
when he finally realized that crossing that road
for so many years
just wasn't funny anymore.

Find the belly-dancing Jell-O and dying buffalo.

The drug addict, turned sex addict, turned food addict,
turned gym addict.
Find the homeless man consumed by a plague of peace,
the body bag and busted shopping bag,
the once-huge heart now turned into a tiny nest of tears.

Find, find, find them all and they'll say...

Find the holy temple,
the gun pressed to your temple,
the Double Bubble, double trouble,
bubble in the bloodstream.

Find the hanging party and garden party,
the deathbed prayer and crystal stair.
The clock that repeatedly strikes the hour of rage,
the most wished-upon star,
the joy deflator hooked up to a re-motivator.

Find the riverdancing Jesus and hula-hooping Buddha,
the lotus flower Happy Hour.
The millions of wallflower angels unable to dance
on the head of a pin,
but still having a kick-ass time at the party.

Find, find, find them all and they'll say:

"Dude, getting caught shoplifting's one thing,
but getting caught shoplifting herpes medication,
glow-in-the-dark strawberry-flavored condoms,
and a clearance-sale book of Sudoku puzzles...

Man, that's some messed-up shit."

No Animals or Insects Were Tortured or Killed In the Making of this Poem

What I want: to crank creation's contrast knob to fully illuminate what's right about the world.

I wanna be Faith's strung-out junkie. My dreaming veins singing a better tomorrow.

What I don't want: to be dust, rust. Roadtripping with demons—Oblivion or bust.

Don't wanna be that one suicide bullet locked and loaded in the chamber of grief's gun. Don't wanna be your blood-lusting grave, your ghost-moan grave, your any kinda grave.

What I want: to spend time in your joy's city. I'll sweep the streets, round up criminals, direct traffic—anything and everything to keep your bliss vibrant and alive.

I wanna radioactivate, self-immolate. Burn away all poverty, fear and sickness to fuel the fire of our well-being.

Don't wanna be an inert gas in the Idiotic Table of Elements. Wanna be a full-on kick in the balls to ignorance.

Never wanna torture or kill any animals or insects in the making of these words, these beliefs, no matter how low I may get between thought, between breath, between life and death.

But if anything must die, let it be the ego. Let it go.

What I want: for you to write on my flesh everything you see and hear when you sleep. Wanna believe the pen outlasts the blade. Freedom outlasts the chains.

I wanna shred your self-doubt, refold it into a confident origami.

Wanna see you go out into the night, take a deep breath. Sip in stars, planets, moonbeams. Let me visit the solar system in your head. Let me be asteroid, nebula. Let us become the Universe of We.

Don't wanna be old news, worn-out shoes, poorly played blues. Don't wanna be a perpetual cruiser up and down the Boulevard of Bad Vibes.

I wanna shake our collective birthright of shame, blame.
Want the veins in my hands to be Sanskrit letters spelling out the words: "I will hold you up when you're down."

I wanna believe that had we lived in the Warsaw Ghetto we would've been survivors. We would've been books for all to read in the secret libraries.

I want our hearts and minds to unite and revolutionize. Never want racism's fist to be supersized.

Finally, I want every sacred word in every language—dead and alive—to be your first and last name. So whenever I call out to you, it feels like I'm praying.

With This Kiss

With this kiss
there are revelations tattooed upon our lips;
revelations more easily read
on account of this silent pact with recognition
where I am beginning to see that we
are slowly becoming healed.

This is not some medicine show down by the river.
I am not faking it, mistaking it, trying to
rake in the bucks
from selling you some snake oil of unfortified conviction.

Just listen.

I offer you no forensic apology.
This is my true astrology–
    beneath the constellation of this revelation
    my head is buzzing like dreaming bees,
stinging me with needles of possibility.

Suddenly I find myself
unallergic to this disease of need.
    I'm ready to move beyond that song I sang:
    a death chant of a soul enslaved.

Ready to move through that Middle Passage
of fear's damnation,
on my way to that Emancipation Proclamation–
    that rock & roll station of this body-nation, singing:

"Holy, holy, whole and hold me."

And the things that happen to deny, to defy,
wherein the laboratory of childhood
we are sometimes made Frankenstein
instead of Frankincense.

Yeah, I know it don't make sense.

Still, I don't want to make this DNA sound DOA.
So I will light a candle for this newly born revelation,
this elation with a holiness localized behind the eyes—
a shine like fire telling stories
the Bible never got quite right.

A regenerative Genesis
where the muscle memory of love is
    bending, stretching, remembering movements
        enacted in passion
that lead me to believe
    heaven is right here
    in the way we are
    with each other in this moment.

Yeah, I heard it through the grapewine,
those spirits speaking to me in double time,
    a hundred proofs of truth saying
    everything's gonna be fine—
Satchmo trumpet whine.

If you're having any trouble hearing it,
tasting it in your mouth like spearmint,
    well here, it's like I said
be-four score and seven years ago—

With this kiss
there are revelations tattooed upon our lips;
revelations more easily read
on account of this silent pact with recognition
where I am beginning to see that we
are slowly becoming healed.

we voice sing

for Phillip Levine

born from new york city rooftops & appalachian mountains / from steady-handed surgeons & nightshift press operators / from refrigerator hum & harmonica hum / from the summer of love & nuclear winters / from puppy love & wolf howl / cobaine & coltrane / graceland to teenage wasteland / we voice grow

born from deejays spinning & dts dizzying / from earthquakes, hurricanes & heartache / four-leaf clovers & coffee breaks / from the last laugh to the first man on the moon / pagan gods & diamond dogs / jeffrey dahmer & the suicide bomber / from tiny town to the motor city / we voice rise

born from childhood schemes & alien transmission machines / from busted-down tenements to wide-open arms waiting for love / from heavy metal / well-worn st. christopher medals / sudden summer downpours & wrecking-ball snores / from the wailing wall to the wonder wall / from the *call of the wild* to girls gone wild / we voice feed

born from barren fields & pregnant pauses / double dates & double indemnity clauses / from lucky cats & muskrat love / 20 volts to lightning bolts / hoboken to holy smokes / desolation row to goodbye yellow brick road / from the wizard of oz & that dear john letter from god / we voice stand

born from failure & faith / crack cocaine & cornflakes / gigabytes & troglodytes / the deep blue sky & hospital flatlines / sticky wickets / winning lottery tickets / muscle cars & cuban cigars / freedom fighters & folk guitars / we voice live

born from the dead of night to the light within / mortal kombat / mortal sin / cold feet / global warming / cadillacs & zodiacs / laid-off saints & hired killers / mother teresa to "this is thriller" / closed minds & open roads / lady di & lady day / brave new worlds to new world order / from your own backyard to across the universe & across the border / we voice sing

we voice grow / we voice rise / we voice feed / we voice stand / we voice live / we voice sing

we voice grow / we voice rise / we voice feed / we voice stand / we voice live / we voice sing

end

Photo by Cat Gwynn

Rich Ferguson *has performed across the country and has shared the stage with Patti Smith, Wanda Coleman, Exene Cervenka, T.C. Boyle, Loudon Wainwright, Bob Holman, and many other esteemed poets and musicians. He has performed on The Tonight Show, at the Redcat Theater in Disney Hall, the New York City International Fringe Festival, the Bowery Poetry Club, the South by Southwest Music Festival, the Santa Cruz Poetry Festival, the DocMiami International Film Festival, the Topanga Film Festival, and Stephen Elliott's "Rumpus." He is also a featured performer in the film, What About Me? (the sequel to the double Grammy-nominated film 1 Giant Leap), featuring Michael Stipe, Michael Franti, k.d. lang, Krishna Das, and others. He has been published in the LA TIMES, has been anthologized by Uphook Press (gape-*

seed), Smith Magazine (The Moment), TNB Books (The Beautiful Anthology), spotlighted on PBS (Egg: The Art Show), and was a winner in Opium Magazine's Literary Death Match, LA. Ferguson is a Pushcart-nominated poet, and also a regular contributor and poetry editor to the online literary journal, The Nervous Breakdown.

More about the author –

"If you've ever seen Rich Ferguson perform, then you know what it's like to sit there in your chair as he stands before you and contorts his body in ten different directions and his eyes roll back into his head as he recites a 2,000-word poem from memory without the slightest slip of the tongue. You understand the energy, the heart, the pain, the electronic angst, the joy. And now, thank god, we have him in print. This collection is lightning in a bottle."

- Brad Listi, author of *Attention. Deficit. Disorder.* and founding editor of The Nervous Breakdown

"Rich Ferguson is gasoline frenzy. A voice challenging the skies, the dirt, the whisky bones, the urbane and the ordinary, the self, the loved, the half-loved, the unloved, the feared and despised. These are poems that kick inside the reader. Here is a voice refusing to settle to dust or rust."

- Jane Ormerod, Author of *Welcome to the Museum of Cattle*

"Like some kind of poetic imp, Rich Ferguson soars courageously through the black hole of language, rescuing the most authentic words of hope, absurdity and passion. There is no end to his infinite reach, and love echoes in his every fierce and wild cry."

- Suzzy Roche, founding member of The Roches and author of *Wayward Saints.*

“Rich Ferguson's work is exquisitely beautiful, deeply compelling, full of the Earth's music and constellations, truly amazing, very highly recommended.”

- Ellyn Maybe, L.A. Poet

“There is a dirty rushing river of blood, bones, styrofoam and stars streaming through the jacked-open church doors of Rich Ferguson’s work; it is here we are transported at unfathomable speeds down tributaries of wretched salvation floating splintered yet centered, crowned heads just above the bubbling water, giving us reason to believe both that there *is* a Unanimous Heart and that this heinous pop culture *is* actually worthy of transcendent prayer.”

- Milo Martin, Californian poet, author of *Poems for the Utopian Nihilist*

“Rich Ferguson is a poet as generous at the microphone as he is on the page. His is poetry "For those who speak from the heart even when it's broken." And in *8th and Agony*, Ferguson splays wide the beast of the matter, digs around for what is lurking there, and sets it out in the sun to be restored. Here he gathers the "fractured rapture" of common words and pieces them together in verses of "limitless exquisiteness." This book rides the ramp between beauty and brutality, and all that is learned in between. I can highly recommend it.”

- Peggy Dobreer, author of *In the Lake of Your Bones*

Other Books from Punk Hostage Press –

'Fractured' (2012) by Danny Baker

'Better Than A gun In A knife Fight' (2012) by A. Razor

'The Daughters of Bastards' (2012) by Iris Berry

'Drawn Blood: Collected Works from D.B.P.Ltd.,
1985-1995' (2012) by A. Razor

'impress' (2012) by C.V. Auchterlonie

'Tomorrow, Yvonne' (2012) by Yvonne De la Vega

'Beaten Up Beaten Down' (2012) by A. Razor

'miracles of the BloG: A series' (2012)
by Carolyn Srygley-Moore

'Small Catastrophes in a Big World' (2012) by A. Razor

Made in the USA
Charleston, SC
04 February 2013